The Godhead Under Siege

A Call for Unity in the Seventh-day Adventist Church in the Face of Division Over the Godhead Issue

By

Lemuel Valendez Sapian

The Godhead Under Siege : A Call for Unity in the Seventh-day Adventist Church in the Face of Division Over the Godhead Issue

Copyright © 2024 by Lemuel V. Sapian.

All rights reserved. Printed in the United States of America. No part of this book may be used or reproduced in any manner whatsoever without prior written permission from the Publisher.

For information contact :

BRIMINGSTONE PRESS

www.brimingstone.press

Book and Cover design by Lemuel V. Sapian
ISBN: 978-1-953562-10-4
First Edition: February 2024

10 9 8 7 6 5 4 3 2 1

Table of Contents

Introduction 10

A Call for Unity 15

Why is Unity Important? 25

Implications for Seventh-day Adventists Today 31

Unity is Essential to the Adventist Faith 34

What is the Trinity? 37

Primary Objections 44

Appendix 73

About the Author 80

The Godhead Under Siege:

A Call for Unity in the Seventh-day Adventist Church in the Face of Division Over the Godhead Issue

Introduction

Dear fellow church leader and members,

I appeal to you in the spirit of unity to face with me one of the issues dividing congregations—and even families—today.

In the sanctuaries of Seventh-day Adventist churches, where the echoes of hymns and prayers have resonated for generations, a profound dilemma has emerged, threatening to disturb the harmonious unity that has long defined this movement. This issue aims at the very heart of our understanding about who God is, challenging the unity that has been a cornerstone of the Seventh-day Adventist Church since its inception. I am referring to the doctrinal divisions surrounding the Triune Godhead, especially when iterated as the "Trinity". This issue has sparked passionate discussions and fervent debates, casting shadows on the unity that has been a beacon of light for so many.

As the winds of theological discourse swirl, carrying with them the weight of divergent perspectives, it is crucial for us, the faithful stewards of Biblical truth, to pause and reflect on the essence of our shared beliefs. It is imperative that we do not be brought away by "every wind" of doctrine. In this shared introspective journey, we must confront the complexities of our doctrinal differences, seeking not division but a deeper understanding that can fortify the bonds that tie us together. It is within this context that we embark on a path to explore the significance of unity within the Seventh-day Adventist Church, particularly when faced with the intricate challenges posed by the often-fiery debates surrounding the Triune Godhead.

The very foundation of Seventh-day Adventism rests on the pillars of biblical truth, prophetic insight, and a commitment to spreading the message of the hope of Christ's soon return to a world in need. However, in our pursuit of doctrinal purity and Biblical truth, we find ourselves at a crossroads where interpretations of the nature of God threaten the very essence of our shared mission. This is not a call to dilute our theological convictions; rather, it is an impassioned plea to recognize that amidst our doctrinal diversity, the call to unity remains a non-negotiable imperative.

Seventh-day Adventists, bound by a common heritage and a shared commitment to the principles illuminated by the prophetic insights of Sister Ellen G. White, have weathered storms of controversy in the past. From the Great Disappointment to the challenges posed by changing times, the strength of our fellowship has been tested and proven. Now, as we grapple with the intricacies of understanding the Triune Godhead, we must draw upon the reservoirs of patience, humility, and love that define our faith tradition. As I was once a lay leader for some time in the church, I have seen these theological disputes firsthand. They have been the cause of much church disunity and disarray.

In addressing the delicate matter of the Godhead, it is paramount to recognize that divergent perspectives do not necessarily equate to a departure from the fundamental tenets of our faith. Rather, they present an opportunity for dialogue, for an exchange of ideas that can lead to a more comprehensive understanding of the divine mysteries that have captivated the minds of theologians and believers throughout the ages. The unity we seek is not one of uniformity but a unity that transcends differences, bound together by a common commitment to the truth as revealed in the Scriptures.

However, with that being said, we must also be cognizant that it is the nature of a movement to be identified by the boundaries that define our faith. It is not merely sufficient to claim one's faith is based on the Bible, for many have different approaches and interpretations; we need a hermeneutical method that allows the Bible to be its own interpreter.

As individual churches navigate the challenging terrain of doctrinal discussions, it is essential to foster an environment of openness and respect. The Apostle Paul, writing to the Corinthians, admonished, "I appeal to you, brothers and sisters, in the name of our Lord Jesus Christ, that all of you agree with one another in what you say and that there be no divisions among you, but that you be perfectly united in mind and thought" (1 Corinthians 1:10, NIV). These words resonate across the centuries, reminding us that the pursuit of unity is not a contemporary challenge but a perennial call to fidelity.

In our pursuit of theological clarity, we must guard against the temptation to let doctrinal differences become stumbling blocks to unity. The fabric of the Seventh-day Adventist Church is woven with threads of diverse perspectives, each contributing to the rich tapestry of our collective understanding. It is within this diversity that the beauty of our faith shines most brilliantly, reflecting the manifold wisdom of God that transcends our finite comprehension.

Amidst the complexities of the Triune Godhead debates, we must remain anchored in the foundational principles that have guided our faith community through the ages. The Seventh-day Adventist Church, with its prophetic heritage, is uniquely positioned to navigate the turbulent waters of theological discourse. We are called not only to articulate our beliefs with clarity but also to embody the spirit of Christ in our interactions, recognizing that our unity is a powerful testimony to the transformative power of the Gospel.

In the following chapters, we will delve into the historical roots of Seventh-day Adventist theology, exploring the various perspectives on the Triune Godhead that have emerged over time. Through this exploration, we aim not to fuel the fires of discord but to illuminate the common ground that unites us. It is our hope that by understanding the historical context and theological nuances surrounding this issue, we can foster an atmosphere of mutual respect and genuine dialogue within our congregations.

As we embark on this journey, let us remember that our shared commitment to the Three Angels' Messages—the heart of our prophetic mission—transcends theological intricacies. The

Seventh-day Adventist Church is called to proclaim the everlasting Gospel, calling people to worship the Creator and anticipate the imminent return of our Lord and Savior, Jesus Christ. In the face of doctrinal challenges, let us not lose sight of this sacred mission that unites us in purpose and destiny.

In the pages that follow, may we find inspiration and guidance to navigate the currents of theological diversity with grace and humility. May we emerge not as a fractured body but as a united force, fortified by the recognition that, despite our differences, we are bound together by a common faith and a shared hope. For in our unity, we reflect the very nature of the God we worship—a God who is love, grace, and the source of all true harmony.

A Call for Unity

In the solemn gathering of Seventh-day Adventist congregations, where the voicing of earnest prayers and the rustle of pages turning in well-worn Bibles echo, a profound truth resonates: *unity is the strength of the church*. These words, inspired by the prophetic insights of Ellen G. White, serve as a rallying cry for a faith community grappling with the complexities of doctrinal discussions, urging us to maintain our unity on common points of our faith.

> "Unity is the strength of the church. Satan knows this, and he employs his whole force to bring in dissension. He desires to see a lack of harmony among the members of the church of God. Greater attention should be given to the subject of unity."
>
> —*E.G. White, 16LtMs, Ms 14, 1901, par. 32.*

As we embark on a journey to understand the urgency and importance of church unity within the Seventh-day Adventist tradition, we must heed the admonition of Ellen White, recognizing that our collective strength is imperiled when dissension infiltrates the sanctuary of our shared beliefs.

> "Satan knows this, and he employs his whole force to bring in dissension..."

These poignant words from Ellen G. White encapsulate the spiritual battle that rages within the Seventh-day Adventist Church. It is a battle not against flesh and blood but against the principalities and powers that seek to sow discord among the faithful. The issue at hand, the nuanced debates surrounding the nature of the Triune Godhead, has become a battleground where the forces of disunity threaten to erode the very foundation of our faith.

Ellen White's insights into the schemes of the adversary remind us that unity is not a mere suggestion but a spiritual imperative. The urgency to fortify the bonds of fellowship within the Seventh-day Adventist Church is emphasized by the realization that Satan's arsenal is most potent when aimed at creating division among believers. In recognizing this, we are compelled to ask ourselves: Why does unity hold such paramount importance, and how can we cultivate it in the face of dissension?

The Biblical Mandate for Unity

The call for unity within the body of Christ is not a novel concept; it echoes through the pages of the New Testament, where the apostles passionately urged believers to maintain the unity of the Spirit in the bond of peace (Ephesians 4:3, ESV). The early Christian communities faced diverse challenges, including cultural differences, theological disputes, and varying spiritual giftings. However, the apostolic injunctions echo with a timeless truth: unity is not a luxury but a divine mandate.

In the Seventh-day Adventist Church, this biblical mandate takes on heightened significance. Our mission, anchored in the prophetic insights of Ellen G. White, is to proclaim the Three Angels' Messages—a message that transcends denominational boundaries and cultural distinctions. The urgency of our mission demands a united front, where the diverse gifts and perspectives within the body contribute to a harmonious symphony that resonates with the truths of God's Word. This mission cannot be realized if dissension is within our ranks.

Navigating Doctrinal Diversity with Humility

The Trinity, a doctrinal cornerstone for many Christian traditions, has become a focal point of discussion and, at times, contention within the Seventh-day Adventist Church. Ellen White, in her writings, emphasized the importance of humility as a safeguard against the divisive influences that seek to exploit doctrinal differences.

> "If the people of God derive spiritual enlightenment from God, they will, in diversity, and as branches of the True Vine, show that unity that Christ has enjoined upon them. If they are humble, they will appreciate the words of Christ, which enjoin humility and unity. They will cherish Christian affection, banishing sloth and lukewarmness. They will draw nigh to God, earnestly interceding for the grace that will give them efficiency and success in representing Christ."

—*E.G. White, 13LtMs, Lt 5, 1898, par. 31*

The apostle Paul, writing to the Corinthians, exhorted believers to be "of the same mind, having the same love, being in full accord and of one mind" (Philippians 2:2, ESV). This call to unity is not a call to forsake our deeply held convictions but an invitation to approach doctrinal discussions with a spirit of humility, recognizing the limits of our finite understanding. Humility opens the door to genuine dialogue, where the exchange of ideas becomes a journey toward collective enlightenment rather than a battlefield of conflicting egos.

The Strength of Unity in Witness and Service

Ellen G. White's assertion that "greater attention should be given to the subject of unity" points to a need for intentional and sustained efforts to foster unity within our congregations. The strength of unity extends beyond the walls of our churches; it resonates in our witness to the world and our collective service to humanity. A united Seventh-day Adventist Church is a powerful force for good, a living testimony to the transformative power of the Gospel.

Jesus, in His high priestly prayer recorded in John 17, expressed His desire for the unity of His followers:

> "I do not ask for these only, but also for those who will believe in me through their word, that they may all be one, just as you, Father, are in me, and I in you, that they also may be in us, so that the world may believe that you have sent me."
>
> —John 17:20-21, ESV.

The unity of believers, according to Jesus, serves as a compelling witness to the authenticity of His mission and the divine origin of the Gospel.

In a world marked by division, strife, and discord, the Seventh-day Adventist Church stands as a beacon of hope when united in purpose. Our mission to share the everlasting Gospel and prepare a people for the soon return of Christ is most effective when we stand together, shoulder to shoulder, proclaiming a message that transcends the temporal concerns that often divide humanity. Unity amplifies our voice, magnifying the impact of our collective witness to a world in desperate need of the hope we profess.

Overcoming Challenges to Unity

While the call to unity is clear, the path to achieving and maintaining it is fraught with challenges. Doctrinal differences, cultural disparities, and varying interpretations of scripture can create tensions that threaten to fracture the unity of the body. However, the acknowledgment of these challenges is not a cause for despair but an opportunity for growth and transformation.

1. *Open and Honest Dialogue*: The Apostle Paul, in his letters to the early Christian communities, modeled a commitment to open and honest dialogue. He engaged with differing perspectives, addressing theological questions and pastoral concerns with grace and clarity. Likewise, Seventh-day Adventist congregations must create spaces for respectful dialogue, where members feel free to express their views without fear of judgment.

2. *Cultivating a Culture of Love*: Love, as articulated in the teachings of Jesus, is the adhesive that binds the body of Christ

together. The Apostle Paul, in his famous treatise on love in 1 Corinthians 13, emphasized that love is patient and kind, not easily angered, and keeps no record of wrongs. A culture of love within Seventh-day Adventist churches provides a fertile ground for unity to flourish, where genuine care for one another transcends doctrinal differences.

3. *Embracing Diversity*: The diversity within the Seventh-day Adventist Church is a strength that should be celebrated rather than feared. Different cultural backgrounds, theological perspectives, and spiritual giftings enrich the fabric of our faith community. Embracing diversity requires a commitment to learning from one another, recognizing the beauty in our differences, and yet upholding to fundamental identifiers and boundaries of our faith.

The Eschatological Significance of Unity

As Seventh-day Adventists, our understanding of last-day events and the eschatological narrative imparts a unique urgency to the call for unity. The Three Angels' Messages, proclaiming the everlasting Gospel, stand as a final warning to a world hurtling towards its ultimate destiny. In this context, the unity of the Seventh-day Adventist Church becomes not only a reflection of our faithfulness to biblical truths but a strategic imperative in fulfilling our prophetic mission.

Ellen G. White, in her visions and writings, provided insights into the climactic events preceding Christ's second coming. As we contemplate upon the approaching apocalyptic panorama, the urgency of our mission grows in intensity. A fragmented, disunited church stands as a stumbling block to the swift proclamation of the Everlasting Gospel to every nation, tribe, language, and people—the very mission entrusted to Seventh-day Adventists.

A Call to Action: Strengthening Unity in the Seventh-day Adventist Church

The urgency and importance of church unity within the Seventh-day Adventist tradition demand a collective commitment to intentional, prayerful action. As we respond to Ellen G. White's call for greater attention to the subject of unity, here are actionable steps that individual churches can take to finish the work of the Gospel:

1. *Prayerful Seeking of Understanding*: Encourage members to engage in prayerful study and contemplation of the doctrinal issues at hand. Create opportunities for small group discussions, allowing individuals to share their perspectives and learn from one another in an atmosphere of humility and respect.

2. *Education and Awareness*: Foster a culture of continuous learning within the church community. Provide resources, seminars, and workshops that delve into the historical, theological, and biblical aspects of the Triune Godhead debate. Equip members with the knowledge needed to navigate these discussions with clarity and wisdom.

3. *Pastoral Leadership and Guidance*: Pastors and church leaders play a pivotal role in shaping the culture of the church. Model humility, transparency, and a commitment to unity in your leadership. Provide pastoral guidance that promotes a balanced understanding of doctrinal issues and encourages congregants to prioritize unity without compromising their convictions.

4. *Community-Building Initiatives*: Organize events and activities that foster a sense of community and belonging within the church. Shared experiences, fellowship, and mutual support contribute to the development of strong interpersonal relationships, forming the bedrock of a united congregation.

5. *Collaborative Outreach Efforts*: Emphasize the collective mission of the Seventh-day Adventist Church in reaching the world with the Three Angels' Messages. Engage in collaborative outreach efforts that underscore the power of a united church in impacting local communities and sharing the hope found in Christ.

6. *Conflict Resolution Strategies*: Develop and implement effective conflict resolution strategies within the church. Train leaders and members in communication skills, active listening, and the art of navigating disagreements with grace and love. A church that handles conflicts biblically and redemptively is better equipped to maintain its unity.

7. *Intentional Discipleship*: Prioritize intentional discipleship programs within the church. As members grow in their understanding of the Gospel and deepen their relationship with Christ, they are more likely to approach doctrinal discussions with a spirit of humility and unity.

All these can be done when we overcome the hurdle of divisiveness that threatens our church on points of doctrine.

A United Church, A Resilient Faith

The call to unity emerges as a vibrant motif in the annals of Seventh-day Adventist history. It is interwoven with threads of prophetic insight and unwavering commitment to truth, with

Ellen G. White's admonition echoing through the corridors of time. It beckons us to recognize that unity is not merely a peripheral concern but a central strength of the church. As we contend with the complexities of the Godhead debates, let us heed her counsel and elevate the subject of unity to its rightful place in our corporate consciousness.

The urgency and importance of church unity within the Seventh-day Adventist tradition lie not merely in the preservation of organizational coherence but more so in the fulfillment of our divine mission. The Three Angels' Messages resound with a clarion call to worship the Creator and anticipate the imminent return of Christ and demand a united and undivided Seventh-day Adventist Church.

May we, as a faith community, rise to the occasion with a renewed commitment to the principles of unity, humility, and love. In the crucible of doctrinal discussions, may we emerge not as fractured factions but as a united body, steadfast in our devotion to Christ and resolute in our proclamation of the everlasting Gospel. As we navigate the challenges of our time, may the Seventh-day Adventist Church stand as a testament to the strength of unity—a living testimony to the transformative power of a faith grounded in the unchanging truths of God's Word.

"There must be unity among the children of God, and nothing must be allowed to enter that will bring alienation and discord."

—*E.G. White, Review and Herald, July 31, 1894, par. 5*

Why is Unity Important?

Analysis of Ellen G. White's Position on Church Unity in Seventh-day Adventism

Throughout Seventh-day Adventist history, the writings of Ellen G. White stand as a guiding light, illuminating the path of our faith for countless believers. Among the many themes woven into her prophetic messages, the call for unity within the Seventh-day Adventist Church emerges as a common theme. In her day there were still many who chose to write pamphlets denouncing the Seventh-day Adventist Church, some even calling it "Babylon". Ellen White's response to these attacks not only highlights the importance of defending the church against this claim but also shows us the paramount importance of unity as a central tenet of Seventh-day Adventist identity.

Historical Context: The Accusation of Babylon

The backdrop against which Ellen White addresses the accusation of the Seventh-day Adventist Church being Babylon is essential to understanding the urgency and relevance of her words. Throughout its history, the Seventh-day Adventist Church has faced external scrutiny and criticism. Some dissenting voices, both within and outside the church, have labeled it as Babylon—a symbol of spiritual confusion and apostasy.

Ellen White, as a co-founder and prophetess of the Seventh-day Adventist Church, faced the responsibility of defending its integrity and mission. In doing so, she consistently sought to redirect the focus from divisive accusations to the foundational principle of unity, emphasizing the need for cohesion among believers.

Brothers Stanton and Caldwell saw fit to publish a set of pamphlets denouncing the Adventist Church as "Babylon". Thanks to a flurry of disagreements which they had with some of the positions taken by the General Conference, they began their distribution campaign earnestly, copies of which came into the possession of Ellen White herself. Suffice it to say, she was not pleased, and wrote of her sentiments. It was not a light rebuke.

Here is the quote:

> "Those who have published the Loud Cry tract have not consulted me upon the subject. They have quoted largely from my writings and put their own construction upon them. They claim to have a special message from God to pronounce the Seventh-day Adventist Church Babylon, proclaim her fall, and call the people of God to come out of her, and try to make the Testimonies substantiate their theory...Beware of those who arise with a great burden to denounce the church. The chosen ones who are standing and breasting the storm of opposition from the world, and are uplifting the downtrodden commandments of God to exalt them as honorable and holy, are indeed the light

of the world. How dare mortal man pass his judgment upon them, and call the church a harlot, Babylon, a den of thieves, a cage of every unclean and hateful bird, the habitation of devils, making the nations drunk with the wine of her fornication, confederating with the kings and great men of the earth, waxing rich through the abundance of her delicacies, and proclaiming that her sins have reached unto heaven and God hath remembered her iniquities? Is this the message we have to bear to Seventh-day Adventists? I tell you No! God has given no man any such message. Let these men humble their hearts before God, and in true contrition repent that they have even for a time stood by the side of the accuser of the brethren who accused them before God day and night."

—E.G. White, Review and Herald, November 8, 1956, par.1 & 17.

The Emphasis on Unity in Ellen White's Message

The quote under analysis begins with a reproachful tone directed towards those who have proclaimed the Seventh-day Adventist Church as Babylon. Ellen White questions their selective use of the Testimonies, her written revelations, to bolster their claims while neglecting the core message that has been the burden of her message—the unity of the church.

The imagery of an angelic command echoes through her words: "Press together; press together; press together." This repetition emphasizes the urgency and insistence with which the divine call for unity is delivered. It's not a casual suggestion but a compelling directive, emphasizing the critical importance of believers standing united in their faith and mission.

Any attempt to subvert the unity God mandates upon His church, is not the work of the Lord. The constant attacks upon the church by those who would undermine the unity under our Fundamental Beliefs are not doing God's will. Notice that Ellen White herself acknowledges Stanton and Caldwell make judicious use of her writings...but state that they use them to support an erroneous theory: that the Church is "Babylon".

The Principle of Unity and Its Consequences

Ellen White's rebuke extends beyond the accusers to the divisive messages they propagate. She laments that these individuals have failed to quote the admonition about unity and the principle that,

> "In union there is strength and victory; in discord and division there is weakness and defeat."
>
> —E.G. White, 7LtMs, Lt 32a, 1892, par. 18.

This principle encapsulates a profound truth—a truth that, when neglected, results in the weakening of the church.

The consequences of such divisive messages are laid bare in Ellen White's words—they divide the church and put it to shame before its adversaries. Here, she identifies a direct correlation between disunity within the church and its diminished effectiveness in standing against the enemies of truth. The unity of the Seventh-day Adventist Church is not merely a matter of internal harmony; it is intricately linked to the church's witness and impact in the broader world.

Discerning the Working of the Great Deceiver

Ellen White attributes the divisive messages to the deceptive influence of the adversary, stating that in such messages, "is plainly revealed the spacious working of the great deceiver."

—*E.G. White, Experiences in Australia, pg. 100.*

Here, she characterizes the divisive forces as aligning with Satan's agenda, a strategy employed to hinder the church from attaining perfection in unity. The use of the term "spacious working" suggests a broad, calculated effort by the enemy to exploit internal discord for his malevolent purposes.

This acknowledgment of spiritual warfare underscores the gravity of the situation. It frames the call for unity not merely as a human aspiration for organizational cohesion but as a vital aspect of the ongoing cosmic conflict between the forces of good and evil.

The Dangers of Independent Judgment

Ellen White's analysis takes a more pointed turn as she addresses the conduct of those who propagate divisive messages. She identifies a dangerous pattern—an adherence to independent judgment. She accuses these individuals of following "the sparks of their own kindling," suggesting that their initiatives are self-driven, lacking the divine guidance that should characterize the church's collective decision-making.

The metaphor of sparks alludes to small, fleeting ideas that, when pursued independently, can lead to destructive outcomes. Ellen White contends that these individuals "move according to their own independent judgment," indicating a departure from the counsel and collective discernment that should guide the church's trajectory. This independence, she warns, cumber the truth with false notions and theories, leading to a distortion of the fundamental doctrines that define Seventh-day Adventism.

Refusal of Counsel and Unbalanced Minds

A recurring theme in Ellen White's critique is the refusal of counsel. She notes that those who propagate divisive messages refuse the counsel of their brethren, choosing to press on in their own way. This refusal is not merely a rejection of human advice given in godly counsel but, in Ellen White's perspective, a rejection of divine guidance mediated through the collaborative wisdom of the church.

The consequences of such refusal are profound—those who persist in this independent course become, in Ellen White's words,

> "just what Satan would desire to have them—unbalanced in mind."

—Ibid.

Here, she identifies a spiritual danger associated with a lack of receptivity to counsel. The term "unbalanced in mind" implies a departure from spiritual sobriety, indicating a growing vulnerability to the subtle deceptions of the enemy.

Implications for Seventh-day Adventists Today

Ellen White's analysis of the accusation of Babylon and the accompanying emphasis on unity holds timeless relevance for Seventh-day Adventists today. In an era marked by diverse theological perspectives, evolving cultural contexts, and the potential for doctrinal discord, her words resonate as a call to prioritize unity above all else.

1. Unity as a Fundamental Concept:

Ellen White's emphasis on unity as the "burden of her message" elevates it to the status of an important principle of our faith. It is not a peripheral concern but an integral aspect of Seventh-day Adventist identity. We do not hold to a congregational polity like the Baptists do. Where there are Freewill Baptists, Southern Baptists, Fundamentalist Baptists and so on, we are simply Seventh-day Adventists. Today, as discussions on various doctrinal issues persist, her call serves as a reminder that unity is not negotiable—it is at the heart of the church's mission and witness.

2. The Role of Divine Guidance:

The caution against exercising independent judgment reveals the need for a reliance on divine guidance and collaborative discernment. While individual study and understanding are crucial, the refusal to consider the perspectives of fellow believers and church leadership can lead to a distortion of truth and a reliance upon self. This has implications for contemporary discussions within the church, urging Seventh-day Adventists to engage in dialogue with humility and openness to collective wisdom.

3. Recognizing the Spiritual Battle:

Ellen White's acknowledgment of the spiritual battle at play highlights the need for spiritual discernment within the Seventh-day Adventist community. The accusation of Babylon and internal dissension are not mere organizational challenges but spiritual battlegrounds. Recognizing this reality compels believers to approach discussions and disagreements with a heightened awareness of the potential influence of the adversary.

4. Relevance to Doctrinal Discussions:

The context of the accusation of Babylon provides a lens through which to view contemporary doctrinal discussions within the Seventh-day Adventist Church. Ellen White's response underscores the importance of maintaining a balance between doctrinal fidelity and the preservation of unity. While doctrinal clarity is essential, it should not come at the expense of the church's unity, witness, and effectiveness in fulfilling its mission.

5. The Imperative of Counsel and Humility:

The refusal of counsel and the ensuing unbalanced minds caution against an attitude of pride and an overreliance on individual insights. In a global church with diverse perspectives, the call for humility and receptivity to counsel becomes imperative. Ellen White's words challenge Seventh-day Adventists to engage in discussions with a spirit of humility, recognizing the value of collective wisdom and the role of guidance from church leadership.

> "God has a people whom He is leading, teaching, and guiding, that they may teach and lead and guide others. There will be among the remnant of these last days, as there was with ancient Israel, those who wish to move independently of the body, who are not willing to be subject to the body of the church, who are not willing to submit to advice or counsel; but ever bear in mind that God has a church upon the earth, and [to] that church God has delegated power...Men will rise up against reproof; men will despise counsel; men will depart from the faith; men will apostatize; they will want to follow independent judgment. Just as sure as they do this, disaster and ruin of souls will be the result."
>
> —*E.G. White, 5LtMs, Lt 33, 1888, par. 30.*

Unity is Essential to the Adventist Faith

Ellen G. White's analysis of the accusation of Babylon and her fervent call for unity crystallize into a profound message for Seventh-day Adventists. Unity, according to her, is not a peripheral concern but a foundational principle—a principle that is intricately linked to the church's effectiveness in fulfilling its mission and standing against the forces of deception.

As contemporary Seventh-day Adventists navigate the complexities of doctrinal discussions, cultural diversity, and the challenges of a rapidly changing world, Ellen White's words serve as a timeless guide. The call to press together, to recognize the strength in unity, resonates as a clarion call that transcends the pages of history and echoes into the future of the Seventh-day Adventist Church. In heeding this call, believers are not merely preserving organizational cohesion; they are upholding a divinely ordained principle—one that reflects the unity of the Godhead and stands as a testimony to the transformative power of a united, faith-filled community.

In writing this plea for unity, I will make my agenda clear: to safeguard the integrity of the Remnant Church, ensuring its flourishing mission to spread the Gospel worldwide. My ultimate goal is for the Three Angels' Messages to be preached across nations, offering hope in a sin-vanquished universe where suffering is eradicated. Regrettably, the ongoing debate on the Trinity has fractured families—both spiritual and biological ties—shattering relationships and introducing discord where harmony once prevailed.

This book's purpose is transparent. While not aiming to be an exhaustive defense of the Trinity, given the diversity even within Trinitarian circles, it staunchly defends our Fundamental Beliefs—the bedrock of the Seventh-day Adventist Movement. These beliefs define our identity and the organizational structure that serves as the vessel for God's Remnant Church.

Even if you disagree with the current position of the Church on the Godhead, I implore you to read the rest of this volume and consider some of the solutions proposed in this book for the sake of greater unity.

I expect that many who hold to the name "Seventh-day Adventist" hold diverse views, and some may conscientiously disagree with our Fundamental Beliefs, yet we must confront the Godhead issue as it is causing plenty of division. Our Fundamentals, encompassing doctrines like the Sabbath, the imminent return of Christ, the Sanctuary doctrine, and the prophetic authority of Ellen G. White, serve as crucial markers of our faith and define who we are. The same is true regarding our Fundamental Beliefs on the Trinity. They establish how we are a monotheistic faith even though Christ and the Holy Spirit are distinct personalities, and how the triune nature of God works for the salvation of mankind.

Challenges to the Fundamental Beliefs are not new. Some struggle with the concept of a literal six-day creation, aligning more with prevalent scientific perspectives. Others question doctrines like the Sanctuary and the Investigative Judgment, opting for alternative views, as exemplified by the teachings put forward by the late Desmond Ford. It is only natural that similar scrutiny extends to our Fundamental Beliefs regarding the nature of the Godhead and the divine Personalities within it. This book seeks not to suppress such inquiries but to address them within the context of preserving the unity essential for our collective mission and witness, and then posit a solution that would ensure a peaceable co-existence.

What is the Trinity?

In order to understand the heart of the controversy, we must analyze what we mean by the doctrine of the Trinity. Unlike the perceptions of some antitrinitarians, adherents to the Trinity doctrine are not a monolithic group and certainly there are variations of the doctrine that not every Trinitarian will be on the same page on. This will give us more perspective when we visit on why many of the early Adventist Pioneers were critical of the orthodox view.

In Christian theology, few doctrines have elicited as much discussion, contemplation, and at times, contention as the doctrine of the Trinity. It is rooted in the foundational tenets articulated by the Nicene Creed, and stands as a cornerstone of Nicene Christianity, shaping the beliefs of both Protestant and Catholic traditions. Let's navigate through a brief history of the doctrine, and some of the general variations.

Nicene Creed

The Nicene Creed, formulated in 325 AD and later revised in 381 AD at the First Council of Constantinople, serves as a bedrock statement of faith for Nicene Christianity. At its core is the articulation of the Trinity—an understanding of God as one essence subsisting in three distinct persons: the Father, the Son (Jesus Christ), and the Holy Spirit. The creed affirms the co-eternity, co-equality, and consubstantiality of these three persons within the Godhead.

This orthodox formulation seeks to balance the recognition of divine unity with the acknowledgment of the distinct roles and personhood within the Trinity. The Father is the source, the Son is begotten of the Father, and the Holy Spirit proceeds from the Father. The creed affirms the mystery of this triune nature, encouraging believers to embrace it with awe and humility.

Catholic Perspective

Catholic theology, anchored in the teachings of the Magisterium and the tradition of the Church Fathers, upholds the Nicene understanding of the Trinity with distinct emphases and theological developments.

The Catholic Church, through its Magisterium, reaffirms the Nicene Creed as a central statement of faith. The Catechism of the Catholic Church articulates the orthodox Trinitarian doctrine, emphasizing the equality of the divine persons and their unique roles in salvation. The importance of the Trinity is underscored in liturgical expressions, prayers, and sacramental theology.

Despite the constant accusations that the Trinity embraced he Catholic version of the Trinity is different from Protestant perspectives on the Triunity of the Godhead. More information is included below.

Within Catholic theology, there is a unique Marian dimension that accentuates the role of the Virgin Mary in relation to the Trinity. The "Ave Maria" prayer, which incorporates the words "Blessed art thou among women, and blessed is the fruit of thy womb, Jesus," echoes the Annunciation and emphasizes Mary's pivotal role in the Incarnation. In this case, Mary acts as a mediatrix outside of the traditionally accepted Trinity, although she is not considered a "divine" person:

> "Mary's title of mediatrix arises from her cooperation in the Incarnation and in the Redemption of mankind."
>
> —P. Frye (2019, August 19). Mary the "Mediatrix of All Graces." Catholic Answers.
>
> https://www.catholic.com/qa/isnt-calling-mary-the-mediatrix-of-all-graces-contrary-to-the-doctrine-that-jesus-is-the-sole

Eastern Catholic Perspective:

The Eastern Catholic Churches, in communion with Rome, bring an Eastern Orthodox flavor to their Trinitarian theology. Drawing from the rich theological heritage of the East, they maintain a balance between the divine mystery and the personal encounter with God. The Eastern emphasis on theosis, or divinization, influences the understanding of how believers participate in the life of the Trinity.

Protestant Perspectives:

Within Protestantism, there exists a broad spectrum of views on the Trinity, reflecting diverse theological traditions and emphases. While all affirm the basic tenets of the Nicene Creed, nuances emerge in the understanding of the relationships between the divine persons.

We need to realize the traditional Catholic doctrine of the Trinity emphasizes consubstantiality and the filioque clause, underscoring the eternal procession of the Holy Spirit from both the Father and the Son. Catholic theology places significant weight on the authority of church tradition and the Magisterium in interpreting Scripture and defining theological beliefs.

In contrast, Protestants, while affirming the Trinity, prioritize sola scriptura and may not include the filioque clause in their statement of faith, focusing more on the authority of Scripture over tradition. Catholic liturgical practices incorporate Trinitarian worship deeply into Mass and sacramental theology, while Protestant worship services vary in their expression of Trinitarian beliefs but often include prayers and hymns affirming the triune nature of God.

Theological emphasis differs, with Catholic theology highlighting the mystery and transcendence of the Trinity, while Protestant theology may emphasize the practical implications for Christian living and mission, such as the empowering role of the Holy Spirit and relational unity within the body of Christ. Despite these nuances, both Catholic and Protestant traditions affirm the doctrine of the Trinity as a foundational belief central to Christian faith.

Reformed Tradition:

The Reformed tradition, influenced by theologians like John Calvin, places a strong emphasis on the sovereignty of God and soteriology. Within this framework, the Trinity is often approached with a profound reverence for the mystery it entails. Calvin himself delved into the complexities of the Trinity, emphasizing the eternal generation of the Son and the eternal procession of the Holy Spirit from the Father and the Son.

Lutheran Tradition:

Martin Luther, a key figure in the Protestant Reformation, affirmed the orthodox understanding of the Trinity. The Lutheran tradition, rooted in Luther's teachings, echoes the Nicene formulation, emphasizing the equality of the three persons while maintaining their distinct roles in salvation history. Luther's focus on justification by faith coexists with a Trinitarian framework that underscores God's multifaceted, yet distinct nature.

Evangelical Perspectives:

In contemporary evangelicalism, diverse views on the Trinity exist, reflecting a wide range of theological influences. Some evangelicals align closely with Reformed traditions, while others may emphasize experiential aspects of the Holy Spirit's work in the believer's life. The emphasis on a personal relationship with Jesus Christ often intertwines with Trinitarian theology, fostering a dynamic understanding of God's presence and involvement in the world.

Trinitarian theology has been a subject of deep exploration and discussion within Christianity, leading to the development of various models or formulations that attempt to articulate the complex nature of the Trinity. While all Trinitarian models affirm the fundamental belief in one God in three persons—Father, Son, and Holy Spirit—differences in emphasis and nuances exist. Here are some prominent Trinitarian models and their key distinctions:

Latin/Western Trinitarian Model:

Filioque Controversy: One significant difference in the Western model, particularly in Latin Christianity, is the inclusion of the term "Filioque" in the Nicene Creed. This addition asserts that the Holy Spirit proceeds not only from the Father but also from the Son. This has been a point of historical contention between Eastern and Western Christian traditions.

Eastern Trinitarian Model:

Procession of the Holy Spirit: Eastern Christianity, particularly Eastern Orthodoxy, emphasizes the procession of the Holy Spirit solely from the Father. This is in contrast to the Filioque clause in the Western model. Basil the Great, Gregory of Nazianzus, Gregory of Nyssa are theologians from the fourth century who played a crucial role in formulating Eastern Trinitarian theology. Their emphasis on the monarchy of the Father and the consubstantiality of the three persons is foundational to Eastern Orthodox thought.

Social Trinitarian Model:

Social Trinitarianism places a strong emphasis on the distinct persons of the Trinity, highlighting their interpersonal relationships and mutual love. This model often draws parallels between communal life within the Trinity and human relationships. As this model has the least number of unscriptural metaphysical assumptions, it is accepted by many Seventh-day Adventists as the "Heavenly Trio" written about by Ellen G. White. Protestant Theologians like Karl Barth have contributed to a social understanding of the Trinity, emphasizing the relational dynamics between the Father, Son, and Holy Spirit.

Economic/Immanent Trinity Distinction:

This distinction separates the activities and roles of the Trinity in relation to creation and salvation (economic) from their eternal, essential nature (immanent). It acknowledges that while God's actions in the world may be distinct, the divine essence remains undivided. Christian Theologians Karl Rahner and Karl Barth have contributed to the exploration of the relationship between the economic and immanent Trinity. Rahner, for example, coined the term "economic Trinity" to describe God's actions in salvation history.

Modalist/Oneness Pentecostal Model:

Modalism, also known as Oneness Pentecostalism, rejects the classical understanding of three distinct persons in the Trinity. Instead, it asserts that Father, Son, and Holy Spirit are different manifestations or modes of the same divine essence. While considered a "heretical" view of the Trinity, it is the subject of much criticism by several of the Adventist Pioneers. Historically, Sabellianism is associated with the modalist perspective. It was deemed heretical by mainstream Christianity for denying the distinct personhood of the Father, Son, and Holy Spirit.

Primary Objections

The many criticisms of the Trinity rarely focus on its diverse nature, preferring to concentrate on issues like how the "three Persons" equate into One God, and this is what some of the earlier Adventist Pioneers wrote about.

Now, we will discuss some of the most prominent criticisms of the Trinity doctrine raised by critics. Again, this is not meant to be comprehensive, but rather a brief treatise aimed at defending the biblical basis of the Fundamental Beliefs and explaining the best course of action for those who find that they can only agree to disagree.

1. **The Trinity is a Catholic belief.**

The doctrine of the Trinity is also accepted by the vast majority of Protestant denominations and continues to be a major pillar of many Protestant confessions and creeds of faith.

Every so often, however, a meme on social media will pop-up on my feed with an ominous figure of the pope with the symbols of the Trinity, attempting to make a connection between the Roman Catholic system and Trinitarian doctrine. Of course, this imagery is intended for shock effect, and its psychological value cannot be overstated. However, we have to also ask why these same posters fail to do the same with other "Catholic" doctrines such as belief in the Divinity of Christ. Would we dare post a meme that insinuates the error of believing Jesus is Divine by virtue of it being a "Catholic" teaching?

Let us remember that the divinity of Jesus Christ was formally affirmed and defined at the First Council of Nicaea in 325 AD. This ecumenical council was convened by the Roman Emperor Constantine I to address theological controversies within the early Christian Church, particularly the Arian controversy.

The Arian controversy centered around the teachings of Arius, a presbyter from Alexandria, who denied the co-eternity and co-equality of the Son (Jesus Christ) with the Father. Arius asserted that the Son was a created being and, therefore, subordinate to the Father. This theological dispute threatened the unity of the Christian Church.

The First Council of Nicaea aimed to resolve this issue and articulate a clear understanding of the relationship between the Father and the Son. The Nicene Creed, formulated during this council, explicitly affirmed the divinity of Jesus Christ. It stated that the Son is "begotten, not made, of one being with the Father," emphasizing the eternal and uncreated nature of the Son.

The Nicene Creed played a crucial role in establishing orthodox Christian doctrine, and the council's decisions laid the foundation for the understanding of the Trinity—that the Father, Son, and Holy Spirit are three distinct persons yet of the same substance. The Nicene Creed, with later revisions at the Council of Constantinople in 381 AD, remains a central statement of Christian faith in many Christian traditions today.

This fallacy is known as the "Genetic Fallacy", and it is a logical fallacy that occurs when one attempts to discredit or invalidate a belief, idea, or argument based solely on its origin or history. In other words, it rejects or accepts something based on its source rather than its own inherent merits or qualities. In the case of the Trinity doctrine, some argue that its association with the Roman Catholic Church automatically disqualifies it from being a valid biblical teaching. However, this argument neglects to examine the doctrine on its own theological and biblical grounds.

Adventists, like other mainstream Christian denominations, recognize that the doctrine of the Trinity finds its roots in the Bible. While the term "Trinity" may not appear explicitly in Scripture, the concept is derived from various passages that portray the Father, Son, and Holy Spirit as distinct persons within the Godhead. Verses such as Matthew 28:19, where Jesus commands baptism in the name of the Father, Son, and Holy Spirit, underscore this biblical foundation. In the section where we discuss the biblical evidence for the Trinity, we will see how the Bible stands as a witness for the "Heavenly Trio" as the Godhead we are to worship and reverence.

The doctrine of the Trinity did not originate as a later innovation by the Roman Catholic Church. Rather, it was shaped and expressed by early Christian theologians who endeavored to discern and express the biblical portrayal of God as presented by the writers of Scripture. Figures like Athanasius, Tertullian, and Augustine played significant roles in further articulating the doctrine, and the majority of later Protestants affirmed its biblical basis. Rejecting the Trinity solely because of its association with Catholicism is not intellectually sound or fair. Let the teaching stand of its own according to the teachings of Scripture.

2. The Adventist Pioneers were Anti-Trinitarian.

The truth is actually more complicated than this, so we must delve into the nuanced landscape of trinitarianism and anti-trinitarianism within Seventh-day Adventist history. This investigation begins by iterating the second tenet of the church's 28 Fundamental Beliefs, which unequivocally declares the Triune God:

> "There is one God: Father, Son, and Holy Spirit, a unity of three coeternal Persons. God is immortal, all-powerful, all-knowing, above all, and ever present. He is infinite and beyond human comprehension, yet known through His self-revelation. God, who is love, is forever worthy of worship, adoration, and service by the whole creation."
>
> —Beckett, J. (2023, December 27). *What Adventists believe about the Trinity. Seventh-day Adventist Church.*
>
> https://www.adventist.org/en/beliefs/god/trinity/

Doctrinal Development is a Process

In the face of dissent, it is appropriate to have a historical analysis to counter anti-trinitarian claims. It's a plea for conviction grounded in inspiration, encompassing both the authoritative Holy Writ and the illuminating insights of the Spirit of Prophecy—an essential guide for God's Remnant people.

The Adventist Pioneers: A Complex Mosaic of Views

Contrary to claims that anti-trinitarianism was a foundational pillar of the original Adventist faith, historical evidence paints a more nuanced picture. The movement's roots in the Millerite era showed a diversity of views, with figures like William Miller, a Baptist and Trinitarian, standing alongside Joshua V. Himes, an ardent Anti-Trinitarian. Despite their differences, the fervor of their collaborative efforts to preach the Second Advent message overshadowed theological distinctions, and this fact challenges the notion that anti-trinitarianism was a foundational pillar of the faith.

So how did Himes and many other Millerite figures become so ardently opposed to the Trinity? Was it a foundational scriptural truth uncovered along with the Second Advent Message? Or was it rooted in theological assumptions carried by certain individuals into the Millerite movement?

A pivotal element in understanding early Adventist theological views on the nature of God is the influence of the Christian Connexion—a movement that began in 1801 as a reaction to Reformed Calvinist doctrines. Initially indifferent to the conceptions of the Godhead, whether for or against the Trinity, the Connexion gradually gravitated toward anti-trinitarian views, aligning with Unitarians and adopting a very liberal and radical stance for their day and age.

In 1806, Elias Smith, a founding member of the Connexion formally rejected the Trinity doctrine, writing, "As for three persons being one, and one three, it never was, nor never will be". (*Smith, Christian's Magazine, No. V, 1806, p.166.*) It is worth noting that Smith's criticisms of the Trinity are based on a misunderstanding of what the actual Trinity doctrine teaches. Only Modalism teaches that the "three persons" of the Godhead are one "person".

Thanks to the influence of Smith, by 1811, the Connexion had fully rejected Trinitarianism in all its forms. Because of this, they became estranged from their Freewill Baptist brethren (who remained Trinitarian) and began to ally with Unitarians who split off from the Methodist Church. Unitarians derive their name from the insistence that God is only one person, and from the belief that an acknowledgment of divinity for any other person was blasphemous.

By 1826 the Christian Connexion was distributing Unitarian-authored literature (*Gospel Luminary, 1826, p. 48*). Universalism, the idea that everyone will eventually be saved, started gaining ground among the members of the Connexion and the Unitarians. Elias Smith himself wavered back and forth between Connexion views and Universalism.

Once William Miller's message began to spread across New England, Joshua Himes, a prominent member of the Connexion and ardent anti-trinitarian became very interested in the Second Advent movement. Through his influence, Miller's message convinced many Connexion members to join the cause. There where still a myriad of differences between the denominations that formed the Millerite movement, yet their focus remained on preaching the imminent Second Coming, deflecting attention from theological differences.

In the aftermath of the Great Disappointment we saw an even greater influx of former Connexion members into the growing Adventist movement. Influential figures like James White and Joseph Bates, both former Connexioners, brought with them their theological presuppositions on the Godhead, driving the movement towards a distinctly anti-trinitarian slant. It's crucial to recognize this as a mere phase, however, and not a doctrinal pillar as some would suggest. Remember that at this time, the vast majority of Adventists still kept the First day as the Sabbath, and many believed in the immortality of the soul. It wasn't until much later that the fledgling group would refine their theological positions on various issues. In a similar vein, the Adventist outlook on the Godhead would undergo transformation under the guiding influence of several ministers and the inspired messenger of God, Ellen G. White.

As the turn of the 19th to the 20th century approached, a significant shift occurred within Adventism under the guidance of God's inspired messenger. The earlier anti-trinitarian stance, influenced by the Connexion, gave way to a more nuanced understanding of the Godhead. The Adventist movement, far from being doctrinally stagnant, matured in response to divine guidance, challenging the notions of some that anti-trinitarianism was an immutable pillar of the Adventist faith.

Examples of this developing understanding is seen in the denominational flagship publications, such as the Review and Herald, and the Signs of the Times. D. M. Canright, who eventually renounced Seventh-day Adventism, wrote while he was still an Adventist minister:

> "All trinitarian creeds make the Holy Ghost a person, equal in substance, power, eternity; and glory with the Father and Son. Thus they claim three' persons in the trinity, each one equal with both the others. If this be so, then the Holy Spirit is just as truly an, individual intelligent person as is the Father or the Son. But this we cannot believe. The Holy Spirit is not a person."

- D. M. Canright, Signs of the Times, July 25, 1878, Vol. 4, No. 28.

Several ministers would challenge this position, not in the 1980's or even the 1930's as some would insist. Many soon came to realize the Connexion's position on the Godhead was simply unbiblical. They began to see an expanded role for the Holy Spirit, and that He had a distinct Personality and could very well be identified as the Third Person of the Godhead, just as the Trinity doctrine claims.

Some interesting historical quotations that provide clear evidence of this development:

> "Is the work that has been noticed in these articles done by an influence?—There is an influence and a power, it is true; but we should not make the mistake of believing in an influence simply, when we so much need the One who carries the influence and power. The Holy Spirit is Christ's personal representative in the field; and he is charged with the work of meeting Satan, and defeating this personal enemy of God and his government. It seems strange to me, now, that I ever believed that the Holy Spirit was only an influence, in view of the work he does. But we want the truth because it is truth, and we reject error because it is error, regardless of any views we may formerly have held, or any difficulty we may have had, or may now have, when we view the Holy Spirit as a person. Light is sown for the righteous."

- R. A. Underwood, Review and Herald, Vol. 75, Vol. 20, May 17, 1898.

"But now let the mind enlarge to take in some of the eternity of the past. There must have been a beginning of this revelation, a beginning of the work of creation. And this must have been the very beginning of the revelation of that same eternal purpose. Preceding this beginning, there must have been, according to Rom. 16:25, R.V., 'times eternal,' when there were no worlds, no created being, not even an angel; in fact, there were only three beings—God the Father, God the Son, and God the Holy Spirit, these three persons in the Godhead."

– *J. S. Olive, Review and Herald, January 1, 1901, Vol. 78, No. 1.*

"The Spirit is the 'third person of the Godhead,' and therefore has no more beginning of days nor end of life than God Himself. There is no record of father, mother, or pedigree given of the Holy Spirit. As the third person of the Godhead, it is greater than Abraham, and could bless him. The Spirit comes to the world as a representative of Christ, and thus is made like unto Christ."

- *S. N. Haskell, Signs of the Times, February 18, 1905, Vol. 20. No. 7.*

"We fear that many have tried to receive the Holy Ghost as an emotion or an influence, when according to His name and position, given Him by Jesus in introducing Him to the disciples, He should be received as a person. The Holy Scriptures everywhere attribute to Him all the characteristics of a person. He has a name, the Holy Spirit, associated equally with the Father and Son."

- G. B. Starr, *Union Conference Record*, December 31, 1906.

"To comfort them, He said, 'And I will pray the Father, and He shall give you another Comforter, that He may abide with you forever.' He was leaving them, and returning to His Father; but He promised to send them 'another', a personal representative and successor, to take His place in His church on earth, till time should end."

– A. G. Daniells, September 30, 1907, Vol. 22, No. 39

"Let it not be forgotten that the Holy Spirit is the third person in the Godhead. Since ascension of Christ, the Holy Spirit has been His representative and successor in this world...The Holy Spirit does not take Christ's place in the church by displacing Him in the hearts of the people, and drawing their affections to Himself. 'He shall not speak of Himself,' said the Saviour. In all His ministry, the Holy Spirit turns the mind and affections to Him who suffered and died for the world. In this He glorifies the world's Redeemer instead of Himself. And this is what He leads every heart to do in which He abides. In view of these considerations, and many others that could be mentioned, every Christian should cherish this blessed Spirit, and pray earnestly for His abiding presence."

– A. G. Daniells, *Signs of the Times*, October 9, 1907, Vol. 33, No. 41

"A personal Holy Ghost in charge of the work of grace, under God and Christ, as their representative and appointed agent, to accomplish the work of regeneration of man's soul, body, and spirit, will be discounted and made to appear only as an influence. When faith in the trio of the Godhead is destroyed, and the One delegated with authority to resist and conquer man's foe is rejected as naught, we are left to the cruel buffetings of Satan, with no power to resist our adversary."

– R. A. Underwood, Review and Herald, November 21, 1907

"THERE are three Beings in the Godhead: God, the Father; Jesus Christ, the Word; and the Holy Spirit. 'These three are one.' I John 5: 7."

– M. E. Steward, Review and Herald, December 15, 1910, Vol. 87, No. 50

In tracing the historical trajectory of trinitarianism and anti-trinitarianism within Seventh-day Adventism, a dynamic and evolving narrative emerges. One that is vastly different than the revisionist narrative proposed by critics of the Trinity doctrine. The Adventist movement's early diversity, influenced by various theological currents, set the stage for doctrinal shifts and transformations. Rather than our history revealing a static adherence to anti-trinitarianism, the Adventist journey reveals a responsiveness to divine guidance and an openness to doctrinal refinement as time went by. As we navigate this historical analysis, it becomes evident that the Seventh-day Adventist Church, like any dynamic faith community, is marked by a continuous journey of theological exploration and growth.

3. The Trinity is unbiblical.

This is certainly an objection seen all too often. It is an overly simplistic claim and dogmatic in its assertion and does not treat the subject with any fairness. It is true that the term "Trinity" and its traditional claims are not directly spelled out in Scripture. It requires piecing together Scriptural portions together like a puzzle that completes the entire picture. Understandably, not everyone is comfortable with that. But just because we have to take many parts of the Bible instead of a direct statement to make a doctrine doesn't make it *unbiblical*. Adventists have always sought truth by taking Scriptural nuggets of truth and placing them together into coherent theological constructs.

This is most certainly the case with the Sanctuary and Investigative Judgment doctrines which are gleaned from principles found in many different points in Scripture. The Seventh-day Adventist perspective on Health Reform is also an idea gleaned from different Biblical principles. So is the Trinity. All throughout the Bible we see the working of the Father, Son, and Holy Spirit in the plan of salvation.

The theological understanding of the Trinity's role in the salvation of humanity finds support in various passages from the Bible. In exploring this concept, we can turn to several key scriptures that highlight the roles of the Father, the Son, and the Holy Spirit.

The foundational expression of God's love and His initiative in the plan of salvation is encapsulated in John 3:16 (NIV), which states,

> "For God so loved the world that he gave his one and only Son, that whoever believes in him shall not perish but have eternal life."

This verse underscores the Father's love as the impetus behind the redemptive plan.

The role of Jesus Christ as the central figure in the salvation narrative is articulated in passages such as Hebrews 9:28 (NIV):

> "so Christ was sacrificed once to take away the sins of many people; and he will appear a second time, not to bear sin, but to bring salvation to those who are waiting for him."

Additionally, Jesus himself states his mission in Mark 10:45 (NIV),

> "For even the Son of Man did not come to be served, but to serve, and to give his life as a ransom for many."

The involvement of the Holy Spirit in the application of salvation is emphasized in John 16:7-8 (NIV), where Jesus says,

> "But very truly I tell you, it is for your good that I am going away. Unless I go away, the Advocate will not come to you; but if I go, I will send him to you. When he comes, he will prove the world to be in the wrong about sin and righteousness and judgment."

This passage illustrates the Holy Spirit's role in convicting and transforming hearts.

These scriptural references collectively portray the Triune God's harmonious work in salvation: the Father's love, the Son's sacrifice, and the Holy Spirit's application, providing a comprehensive understanding of the Trinity's involvement in the redemption of humanity.

Much of the objection against the traditional doctrine of the Trinity in current day Adventism lies on the nature of Christ's origin and what the Holy Spirit is. On the former, many insist that Christ was "birthed" in some way from the Father. Most modern iterations of anti- and nontrinitarian belief distance themselves from the Arian idea of Christ being a mere creature, created at some point before the world. They prefer to say that Christ was "begotten" and "born" of the Father at some point before the world existed. For them, this absolves them from the counter objection that Christ had a beginning: Christ's life and existence is *derived* and not *given* by the Father. While this obvious play with words and semantics might deceive the unstudious, it is apparent that there is no difference. Humans have life, derived from our Creator via His breath which is within us.

The full nature of the Holy Spirit will continue to be a mystery for us, however, there are enough Scriptural statements that show us that the Holy Spirit is more than just an influence or a divine force emanating from the Father; the Holy Spirit is a divine Person who can be grieved, one who testifies not of Himself, but of Christ. He is Christ's Representative, and acts in Christ's stead on the earth.

The Biblical testimony is abundant and clear that the Holy Spirit is a distinct personality from Christ. We know this because in the Gospel of John, Jesus promises the coming of "Another Comforter" to His disciples. In John 14:16-17 (KJV), Jesus says,

> "And I will pray the Father, and he shall give you another Comforter, that he may abide with you

> forever; Even the Spirit of truth, whom the world cannot receive because it seeth him not, neither knoweth him, but ye know him, for he dwelleth with you and shall be in you."

This promise is significant for several reasons:

Distinct Identity: Jesus speaks of "another Comforter," indicating that this Comforter is separate from Himself. If the Comforter were merely a manifestation of Christ, there would be no need for the term "another." Jesus is a Comforter, and the Holy Spirit is "another Comforter".

Writes Ellen G. White,

> "The Holy Spirit is the Comforter, in Christ's name. He personifies Christ, yet is a distinct personality."
>
> — *E. G. White, 8LtMs, Ms 93, 1893, par. 8.*

Sister White makes it clear that the Holy Spirit is a distinct personality from Christ, just as Christ is a distinct personality from the Father:

> "The oneness existing between the Father and the Son does not affect the distinct personality of each."
>
> — *E. G. White, 19LtMs, Lt 317, 1904, par. 10.*

How does Sister White make this determination? She does so by invoking the evidence found in the Scriptures. In John chapter 16 verse 13 and 14 (NKJV) we find the distinction between Christ and the Holy Spirit thus,

> "However, when He, the Spirit of truth, has come, He will guide you into all truth; for He will not speak on His own authority, but whatever He hears He will speak; and He will tell you things to come. He will glorify Me, for He will take of what is Mine and declare it to you."

Christ references the Holy Spirit as a Person who glorifies Him. With these Biblical pieces in place, we can now see more complete picture. While we should not be presumptuous and think we understand the Godhead fully now that we believe in the Heavenly Trio. The full nature of God will continue to elude the intellect of lowly humanity. But we are at least able to affirm the essential gist of the Trinity, One God in Three Persons. Some will continue to object, "the math doesn't add up", to which we respond, it isn't supposed to make sense. The mystery of the Godhead is not an item that mortal humans can comprehend.

> "For the wisdom of this world is foolishness with God. For it is written, He catches the wise in their own craftiness."
>
> *1 Corinthians 3:19, NKJV*

It must be noted, however, that the Adventist understanding of the Trinity is different from the Classical view of the Trinity. What does this mean? The Classical view sees God as being in a timeless and spaceless realm, whereas Adventism rejects such fanciful philosophical assumptions. We view God as within the spatiotemporal realm, God interacts with us in a very real and historically verified way. We agree somewhat with Karl Barth's understanding of a social Trinity, a Godhead of Three Persons who share in one love and purpose and tend to leave the other metaphysical additions of philosophical thought as speculative and unneeded in our understanding of who God is.

Nonetheless, we remain steadfast in our defense of the Triune Godhead as it is revealed in Scripture. God does not reveal everything about Himself, but we are given enough information to make a solid doctrinal teaching.

As a side note, the issue of the *Johannine Comma* can be discussed.

The Johannine Comma, found in 1 John 5:7-8, is a disputed passage within the New Testament that has sparked significant scholarly debate. The Comma reads:

> "For there are three that bear record in heaven, the Father, the Word, and the Holy Ghost: and these three are one. And there are three that bear witness in earth, the Spirit, and the water, and the blood: and these three agree in one."

This passage, if authentic, provides explicit support for the doctrine of the Trinity, affirming the unity of the Father, Son (referred to as "the Word"), and Holy Spirit as one.

However, numerous scholars and textual critics question the authenticity of the Johannine Comma for several reasons. One primary concern is the absence of this passage in the earliest Greek manuscripts of the New Testament. Manuscripts such as *Codex Sinaiticus* and *Codex Vaticanus*, which date from the 4th century, do not include the Comma. Additionally, many later manuscripts that do contain the Comma show signs of interpolation or alteration, suggesting that it may have been inserted into the text at a later date.

Furthermore, the style and vocabulary of the Johannine Comma differ from the rest of the First Epistle of John, raising suspicions about its authorship and originality. The passage appears to interrupt the flow of thought in the surrounding verses and lacks the characteristic Johannine language and themes found elsewhere in the epistle.

Despite these concerns, some scholars argue that there is evidence to suggest that the Johannine Comma may indeed be an authentic part of the original text. One line of evidence comes from the Latin Vulgate, a translation of the Bible into Latin completed by Saint Jerome in the late 4th century. The Comma is present in the Vulgate manuscript tradition, indicating that it was known and accepted by some early Christian communities.

Furthermore, historical records suggest that the Johannine Comma was cited by several early Christian writers, including Cyprian of Carthage and Priscillian of Avila, in the 3rd and 4th centuries. While these references do not prove the authenticity of the Comma, they provide evidence that the passage was known and used by some early Christians.

Additionally, the presence of the Johannine Comma in certain manuscripts associated with the Waldensian movement, suggests that it was part of their biblical tradition. The Waldenses were known for their adherence to the Scriptures and rejection of certain Catholic doctrines, making it unlikely that they would have added a spurious passage to their Bible.

The authenticity of the Johannine Comma remains a topic of debate among scholars and theologians. While its absence from early Greek manuscripts raises doubts about its originality, the presence of the passage in certain Latin manuscripts and its citation by early Christian writers suggest that it may have been part of the original text of 1 John 5:7-8. It is certainly not my desire to speculate further on its authenticity here, only to add an interesting item of further discussion. It is noted that the vast majority of Trinitarian scholars, including those in the Adventist denomination, reject its authenticity. But I will leave the final judgment up to you, the reader. Further research and analysis are necessary to reach a definitive conclusion regarding the status of the Johannine Comma in the New Testament.

4. We should not have a creed.

The Seventh-day Adventist Church does not have creeds. We have Fundamental Beliefs which can and are often amended. We need a set of identifiers that point out the basic beliefs we have as a people. These delineations outline our understanding of what the Bible teaches us and continues to be a way for us to teach others about what we believe.

There are still many variations in theological beliefs among us as Adventists, but the Fundamental Beliefs highlight the very basic ones, including the Sabbath, the Sanctuary, and the State of the Dead. Our belief in the Godhead should be no different. We have retained this Fundamental Belief because it follows the fact that we believe in the full inspiration of the Bible and the prophetic authority of Ellen G. White. Can this belief be revised and even reversed? Why, certainly. This is how the Fundamental Belief on the Trinity came about; we no longer felt the need to confine ourselves to a non-trinitarian stance, but embraced the truth of the Triune Godhead due to the abundance of evidence revealed in Scripture and in the writings of Ellen G. White.

Writes David Trim,

> "While Seventh-day Adventists since 1860 have understood creeds to be unchangeable, they saw statements of fundamental beliefs as being acceptable, partly because they were open to revision. They wanted the freedom to modify their confessional statement so as to reflect more accurately progressive biblical revelation. When the denomination became convinced that one of its beliefs was in error (such as the semi-Arian understanding of the Godhead), Adventists

collectively discerned it appropriate to amend their doctrine of God."

https://adventistreview.org/magazine-article/2103-22/

We have accepted the co-eternality of the Three Persons of the Godhead because we have no Biblical inclination to assume any of them had a beginning—eternality is part of the definition of divinity—and God has underived immortality.

Ellen G. White affirms the co-eternality of the Three Persons (emphasis added):

> "The ETERNAL FATHER is waiting for us to take our eyes off finite man, and place our dependence on him."
>
> – E.G. White, *Review and Herald*, October 16, 1900, par. 5

> "The Word existed as a divine being, even as the ETERNAL SON of God, in union and oneness with his Father."
>
> – E.G. White, *Review and Herald*, April 5, 1906, par. 5

> "The Lord will speak through His messengers. They are only the human instrumentalities, possessing no grace or loveliness of their own, and are powerful and efficacious only as God, the ETERNAL SPIRIT, shall work upon human hearts."
>
> — E.G. White, *7LtMs*, Lt 16j, 1892, par. 9.

Unless there is some good and valid Biblical reason to reject these facts, then the Fundamental Belief on the Trinity should remain as it is, and creating division over it in our churches is both unwarranted and subversive to the unity that God desires for His people.

To wit, the Seventh-day Adventist Church does not have creeds, but we do have revisable Fundamental Beliefs that outline the boundaries of our faith and define who we are.

Trim explains further,

> "The longstanding Adventist claim not to have a formal creed means that we do not have an inflexible statement that defines Seventh-day Adventist beliefs and that cannot be altered, even in minor ways. What we do have are the Fundamental Beliefs, which describe what Seventh-day Adventists have agreed they believe, and which, while they have had the same core throughout Adventism's history, have taken on different forms, have grown in number, and have been expressed in different ways.
>
> We do not have a straitjacket that constrains Bible study, impeding the attainment of a deeper understanding of divine truth. Neither, to extend the metaphor, do we wear a motley, ill-fitting collection of multifarious theological rags. We have a made-to-measure yet flexible garment, well sewn, carefully and lovingly mended over many decades, that helps to protect us from the icy winds of doctrinal incoherence."

In other words, we seek to have a balance which allows us to "Therefore, brethren, stand fast, and hold the traditions which ye have been taught, whether by word, or our epistle.

5. What should I do if I still disagree with the Trinity doctrine?

In the diversity of theological beliefs, divergent interpretations and convictions can sometimes arise within a community. Such is the case within the Seventh-day Adventist Church, where, while the doctrine of the Trinity stands as a cornerstone of faith, it is constantly facing a litany of attacks. I believe this book has given enough reasons for the Adventist Church to maintain its Trinitarian Fundamental Beliefs. Yet, amidst the harmonious general adherence to the fundamental beliefs, there exist individuals who find themselves unable to conscientiously affirm the Trinity doctrine as articulated within the church's Fundamental Beliefs. In light of the importance of unity within the body of believers, it becomes imperative to address this issue with wisdom and compassion.

Ellen G. White, spoke to the dangers of internal discord within the church. She cautioned against those who would turn their weapons against the church militant, emphasizing the need for divine guidance, humility, and a focus on spiritual welfare rather than intra-ecclesiastical strife:

> "When men arise, claiming to have a message from God, but instead of warring against principalities and powers, and the rulers of the darkness of this world, they form a hollow square, and turn the weapons of warfare against the church militant, be afraid of them. They do not bear the divine credentials. God has not given them any such burden of labor."

—E.G. White, *Review and Herald*, October 17, 1893, par. 7.

Indeed, the unity of believers is not merely a matter of organizational coherence but serves as a powerful testimony to the world regarding the truth of the Christian message, and in this present age, the Adventist message proclaimed by the Three Angels.

Sister White's writings underscore the significance of church unity in bearing witness to the transformative power of the gospel. She notes that a harmonious church presents a compelling case for the Christian religion to the watching world. Dissensions and petty conflicts, she argues, tarnish the image of Christ and hinder the church's mission:

> "If the world sees a perfect harmony existing in the church of God, it will be a powerful evidence to them in favor of the Christian religion. Dissensions, unhappy differences, and petty church trials dishonor our Redeemer. All these may be avoided if self is surrendered to God, and the followers of Jesus obey the voice of the church. Unbelief suggests that individual independence increases our importance, that it is weak to yield our own ideas of what is right and proper to the verdict of the church; but to yield to such feelings and views is unsafe and will bring us into anarchy and confusion. Christ saw that unity and Christian fellowship were necessary to the cause of God, therefore He enjoined it upon His disciples. And the history of Christianity from that time until now proves conclusively that in union only is there strength. Let individual judgment submit to the authority of the church."
>
> —*E.G. White, Testimonies for the Church 4:19, 16LtMs, Ms 139, 1901, par. 11.*

Thus, preserving unity within the body becomes a sacred duty, reflecting Christ's injunction for His disciples to maintain fellowship and unity.

Given these principles, what then should Seventh-day Adventists who find themselves at odds with the Fundamental Beliefs on the Trinity conscientiously do? In the interest of upholding both personal convictions and the unity of the church, a path of peaceful resolution is warranted. It is suggested that such individuals, rather than engaging in divisive debates or attempting to reshape the doctrinal landscape of the broader church body, consider forming their own organization.

This proposal may initially seem radical or even counterintuitive, yet it holds the potential for maintaining harmony within the Seventh-day Adventist community. By establishing a separate organization where theological viewpoints align more closely with their individual convictions, dissenting members can find solace and spiritual fellowship without disrupting the unity of mainstream congregations. This approach allows for mutual respect and understanding, affirming the autonomy of conscience while honoring the collective identity of the larger church body…and their own.

Such a course of action reflects the principles of humility, selflessness, and deference to the authority of the church, as advocated by Ellen G. White. Rather than asserting individual independence or fostering anarchy within the ranks, it demonstrates a willingness to prioritize unity and cooperation for the sake of the gospel mission. Once those with conscientious objections form their own corporate body, they can foster a sense of unity focused on the points of doctrine they share. Moreover, it offers a pragmatic solution to the contentious arguing within the church and preserves the liberty of conscience while fostering an atmosphere of mutual respect and cooperation, as with anti- and nontrinitarians having their own organization, they are expected to hold to their own doctrines.

To conclude, the challenge of reconciling personal convictions with the doctrinal standards of the Seventh-day Adventist Church is not an insurmountable one. Through a commitment to humility, understanding, and a shared commitment to the gospel mission, dissenting members can navigate these tensions through creating an identity of their own. By considering the formation of a separate organization aligned with their unique theological convictions, they can find peace and fellowship without compromising the unity of the Adventist church body. In doing so, they uphold the sacred principles of conscience, unity, and Christian love, bearing witness to the transformative power of Christ's message in a world desperately in need of hope and reconciliation.

The front cover image is taken from the mural above the door of the Minneapolis SDA Church seen below, signifying the Trinity Godhead of Father, Son, and Holy Spirit.

The Seventh-day Adventist General Conference meeting of 1888

Appendix

More Quotations from Contemporaries of Ellen G. White Regarding the Trinity/Triune Godhead

"IF it is not a solemn, public, and practical profession of Christianity, WHY should Paul say, 'As many of you as have been baptized into Christ have put on Christ'? Gal. 3:27. IF it is not the solemn profession of our faith in the TRINITY, WHY should Christ command it to be done 'in the name of the Father, and of the Son, and of the Holy Ghost'? Matt. 28:19."

—W.P. Pearce, *Review and Health*, August 2, 1898, Vol. 75, No. 31

"But now let the mind enlarge to take in some of the eternity of the past. There must have been a beginning of this revelation, a beginning of the work of creation. And this must have been the very beginning of the revelation of that same eternal purpose. Preceding this beginning, there must have been, according to Rom. 16: 25, R. V., 'times eternal,' when there were no worlds, no created being, not even an angel; in fact, there were only THREE BEINGS—God the Father, God the Son, and God the Holy Spirit, these three persons in the Godhead."

—H. F. Phelps, *Review and Herald*, January 1, 1901, Vol. 78, No. 1

"Yet if, looking into our faces, watching our daily lives, examining the motives of our every-day actions, they see reflected therein the glory of the Son, the radiance of the Father, and the loving, tender influence of the Comforter, will not they be convinced of the wisdom and love of the TRIUNE GOD? What an incentive to right thinking! What a motive for right living! What opportunities for the silent living out of God's principles! What a privilege of witnessing for the Master we profess to dearly love!"

—*Anna C. White, Review and Herald, January 29, 1901, Vol. 78, No. 5*

"Righteousness is a fruit of the Spirit of God, imparted to man by that divine agent of the TRINITY."

—*G.B. Starr, Bible Echo and Signs of the Times, February 24, 1902, Vol. 17, No. 9*

"A gentleman passing a church one day with Daniel Webster, asked him, 'How can you reconcile with reason the doctrine of the Trinity?' The statesman replied, by asking, 'Do you understand the arithmetic of heaven?'"

—*Uriah Smith, Review and Herald, December 2, 1902, Vol. 79, No. 48*

"THE doctrine of the TRINITY is TRUE when rightly understood. They are one in nature, one in purpose, and so perfect is that union, that Christ said, 'I and My Father are one'."

—*Stephen Haskell, Bible Training School, March 1, 1906, Vol. 4, No. 10*

"In our Doctrinal Bible class we studied some of the leading points of faith COMPOSING THE SYSTEM OF BELIEF OF SEVENTH-DAY ADVENTISTS: e.g., the Power and Inspiration of the Word, the Nature and Character of the TRIUNE GOD, Creation, the Fall, the Plan of Salvation, the First Advent of Christ, the Second Advent, the Sabbath Question in all its phases, the Tithe, the Ordinance of Humility, and the Earthly Sanctuary and its Services."

—*H.C. Lacey, The Missionary Worker, June 6, 1906, Vol. 10, No. 12*

"IF WE FOLLOW THE BIBLE, the Holy Spirit forms one of the TRINITY. There are three that bear witness in earth, the Father, the Word (which is Christ) and the Holy Ghost, and these three are one 1 John 5:8. That which is attributed to God the Father, is attributed to Christ, and what is attributed to God and Christ, either in word or works, is attributed to the Holy Spirit."

—*Stephen Haskell, Bible Training School, June 6, 1907, Vol. 6, No. 1*

"THE Person by Whom God will judge the world is Jesus Christ, God Man. The second Person in the TRINITY, that same Person of Whom we read in our Bibles, Who was born of the Virgin Mary, lived in Galilee and Judea, and was at last crucified without the gates of Jerusalem, will come to judge the world both in His divine and human nature, in the same human body that was crucified, and rose again, and ascended up into heaven."

—Jonathan Edwards, Present Truth, December 24, 1908, Vol. 24, No. 51

"There IS a TRINITY, and in it there are three personalities. We have the Father described in Dan. 7:9, 10, a personality surely—the 'Ancient of Days' enthroned. In Rev. 1 : 13-18, we have the Son described. He is also a personality."

—R. HARE, Union Conference Record, July 19, 1909

Notes

Notes

Notes

About the Author

Lemuel Valendez Sapian is from Denton, Texas and holds a Bachelor's of Arts degree in History from the University of North Texas and studying to earn his Masters in Divinity at the Seventh-day Adventist Theological Seminary at Andrews University. Married to Michelle, together they have four fast-growing children. His passion is for world, religious, American and military historical studies. A lifelong Christian, he is a minister in the Seventh-day Adventist Church, serves in the United States Air Force Chaplain Corps, is a business owner and avid traveler.

www.godhead.quest

www.ingramcontent.com/pod-product-compliance
Lightning Source LLC
Chambersburg PA
CBHW071331040426
42444CB00009B/2132